Dedicated to the Best Parents in the
Universe .. My Own

&

For Maisie .. We are So Proud of You

To Lucky,
My cheerful &
helpful new friend x
Ellen :)

<u>Praise for 'Just Be Yourself'</u>

'Ellen writes with compassion about a subject she knows inside and out through years of working in our High Schools. She has seen aspects of students that are sometimes kept hidden even from parents. She provides an essential guide to help adults towards a more effective understanding of young people at this complicated and vulnerable time of their lives.'

Professor Victoria Door; Head of Department and Director of Keele University's Teacher Training.

'This book serves as timely reminder for parents and professionals to view and understand the world through the eyes of the young person. Ellen uses practical and well thought out advice designed to build confidence, character and wellbeing.'

Professor Dave Putwain AfBPS C.Psychology Liverpool John Moores University

I did then what I knew how to do. Now that I know better, I do better' - Maya Angelou

Forward

When I need sympathy, all I need to do is to mention that I work with teenagers. "*Oh poor you*" they say, "*Kids are so disrespectful these days aren't they? Not at all like we were at that age*". Then I spend yet another hour defending the younger generation, pleading their case all over again. But do you know that in all the years I have worked as a Careers Adviser I am struggling to bring to mind more than a handful of young people who fit the Media's stereotype. True, some are rude or aggressive at times but that is usually an attempt to disguise the inadequacy they feel. Many of them have given up even before they start and feel very negative about their future. Dedicated parents, carers and teachers do their best to help them to navigate the pitfalls along Life's road, but they too can feel overwhelmed when their job description seems to get longer every day.

When my own Mum and I joined forces a few years ago to write an article which we called 'Vitamin P', it really struck a chord with the people who read it. The idea of lavishing praise on young people to boost their self-esteem seemed to be *almost too easy* and the article was well received by people around the world.

I try to use 'Vitamin P' with all the young people I meet and see at first -hand what a difference it makes. My book is a token of the respect I have for the ten thousand or so young people who I have met in my career so far as they never cease to amaze me in their resilience. And while the names have of course been changed, their experiences are *very* real. I have tried to write from my professional point of view as an experienced Careers Adviser and also from being Mum to a teenage daughter. I didn't actually set out for my book to be autobiographical, but it seems to have turned out that way in places! *"Just be yourself"'* is the advice that my parents have given when my confidence has been in short supply, but it has taken me all these years to really understand just what that means.

Contents

Listening to young people's ideas and opinions is so essential in nurturing their self-esteem. Technology has sadly deprived us of too many real conversations and most young people have been completely drawn into its trap. My opening chapter is a reminder of how to get back to basics and listen to each other.

If praise was available on the NHS, millions of us would be prescribed it. Vitamin P (Praise) can make young people feel amazing, but unfortunately lots of adults just don't know how to use it. This chapter suggests simple ways in which we can all be much more lavish with it.

Whatever our age, when we are faced with criticism we all feel deflated. Young people take it so much more personally though and criticism can soon lead to resentment. This chapter explains how to make a Praise Sandwich so that criticism is constructive rather than destructive.

Chapter 4 – Respectfully Yours

Many young people are coping bravely with difficult home lives and personal problems. They deserve our admiration and respect. When we show these, we are setting an example of how they should be treating us.

Chapter 5 - Positive Thinking

Being in control of our own thoughts is the key to feeling strong and resilient, so encouraging young people to think positively can be life changing for them.

Chapter 6 - Becoming an Individual

Learning to 'be yourself' is not quite so easy when you don't actually know who you are yet. Self-awareness evolves with life experiences, but adults can encourage young people to find and then express their uniqueness.

Chapter 7 - Confident Decisions

Knowing how to make a good decision is vital in today's choice-laden world and we all approach them in different ways. The process is a truly fascinating one.

Chapter 8 - Handling Disappointments

Handling the setbacks and obstacles that life throws at us is really difficult. Is it possible to somehow prepare young people for disappointments before they happen though and should we even try?

Chapter 9 – Secure Boundaries

Having clear boundaries helps young people to know where they stand in the world and gives them a feeling of security. This final chapter suggests how to build that strong structure.

"The greatest audience a child can have, is an adult who is genuinely interested in them"
– Walt Disney

Chapter 1: Learning to Listen

On holiday last summer I watched enthralled as an entire family plugged in their headphones, switched on their technology and settled down to ignore each other for the entire afternoon. No-one spoke for more than an hour as they sat by the swimming pool, texting like maniacs and laughing at their own private jokes. If visitors from another planet had landed at that moment they would have ran right back to their spaceship, concluding that Earthlings were completely mad. The sad thing is, they would have been right - we have all gone mad, for Technology. With our playlists, blogs and selfies, who needs other people anyway? Just like Robinson Crusoe, we are stranded in a sea of electronics that has made face-to-face conversations seem like far too much hard work. The knock-on effect is that many young people are finding themselves stranded in a world that has less and less time to listen to them. So they submerge themselves in Facebook or Instagram as a way of getting the attention they need. It wasn't really until I started to train as a Careers Adviser though that I considered listening to be a skill. I thought that if you just grunted and nodded in the right places when someone spoke to you, then that was all there was to it.

Then I started to notice just how many people in my life *really listened* to me without checking their phone, make-up or whether they had spinach stuck in their teeth every five minutes. I was unpleasantly surprised, as the truth is that our world has *so* many distractions that listening properly can be a real challenge. Which is why far too many frazzled parents are guilty of only half listening to their children as they get older, finding it hard to relate to them at all. They might feel comfortable making a fuss of curly haired toddlers but teenagers can feel like a different breed altogether. Instead, conversations revolve around nostalgia as parents harp back to 'how easy it used to be' when their offspring were younger. Which is probably the reason adolescence is called the Awkward Age.

Learning how to be a better listener takes plenty of patience and practise, so when I started training as a Careers Adviser, every Thursday the University would bus in a group of unsuspecting High School students for us to interview. It was a nerve wracking day for everyone involved, as one young man I offered careers guidance to would agree! He was subjected to a deluge of questions from me, before being hit by another one. So I shouldn't have been quite so surprised when after a very l-o-n-g twenty minutes he nearly ran out of the room, tripping over his bag in a bid to escape. Worse was to follow, as we all had to critique each other's interviews at the end of the day, which had all been secretly recorded!

I was *mortified* as we all watched my interview back, but my lecturer Norma just smiled kindly and said *"next time Ellen, don't be afraid of the silences, that is the other person's thinking time"*. Ever since then I have tried to remember that advice and be patient with pauses rather than fill them with babble.

Perhaps the longest pause I ever had happened on a warm afternoon in school when a student called in to see me. Lydia asked for my help in completing her college application form and sat at the desk behind me to do it. After a few minutes it went so quiet that I realized she had fallen fast asleep. When she woke up a few minutes later, she told me that she had slept on her friend's sofa the night before after a huge row with her mum. She had left home and was exhausted physically and emotionally and wanted to talk it through. I listened quietly, the college application form put to one side for the day. When she came back to see me a week later, we sent off the form and she thanked me genuinely. I knew then that putting my own script to one side and just listening instead had been *exactly* the right thing to do.

Some questions help people to talk more easily, while others can lead down a conversation cul-de-sac. 'Open questions' make the other person feel that you are genuinely interested in them and want to hear their answers.

"*How* did your football training go last night?"
"*What* would you like to do at the weekend?"
"*When* can we go Christmas shopping together?"
Closed questions on the other hand can be easily answered with a yes, no or just a grunt:
"*Did you have a good day?'* - "NO"
"*Have you got any homework?"* - "NO".

Try reflecting back on what you think the other person has just said as another technique to make them feel understood. It also gives you the chance to check if you have understood what has been said so far:
"*So what you are saying is…?*"
"*You seem to be finding it hard to talk to Zoe then?*"
"*It sounds like you've been feeling pretty low lately?*"

Perhaps you are the type of person that secretly thinks that 'you know best' most of the time or who have strong opinions about lots of things? If that is the case then improving your listening skills will be good news for the young people in your life. So while it might be a huge effort on your part to bite your tongue, remind yourself of the old saying '*if I want your opinion I will ask for it*'. Welcome *their* ideas, however random they might seem at first. Which is exactly what we learnt to do two years ago when our daughter suggested we went to Scotland on holiday to meet her new Facebook friend. *A mere six hour journey away*. Well naturally we wasted no time in pointing out all the reasons why her idea was not a good one.

So we shouldn't have been at all surprised when she ran upstairs shouting over her shoulder *"You never listen to me!!!"* When we all sat down to talk properly later on, we realised that there was a train that went to Glasgow from Birmingham, our main railway station. She was so pleased that her idea had been taken seriously and she got to meet her new friend.

Unfortunately there are far too many young people who are *not* listened to and Ben was one of these. He pushed past me in the school corridor one morning bright red in the face, rubbing his grazed knuckles. When I called after him to ask if he was okay, he growled something about being *"suspended for three days"*. He was so angry that I made him sit down for ten minutes while he told me what had happened. I listened while he pulled himself together and the next morning when I saw him he muttered an embarrassed *'thank* you' under his breath. When I replied saying that I hadn't really done very much Ben said *"Yes you did Miss - you asked me how I was"*.

SO: *Swap technology for real conversations &*
 Be a genuine and patient listener

"People will forget what you said and forget what you did, but they will never forget how you made them feel."   - Maya Angelou

Chapter 2: Vitamin P

Driving home one evening I found myself absorbed in a discussion on the radio about a new vitamin supplement. The Doctor said it was 'vital for healthy bones' and it started a new train of thought. How amazing if there was a vitamin supplement that could boost young people's self-esteem. The more I thought about it, the more I realised that this already existed - Vitamin P (for praise). Because when we give young people praise, they soak it up like flowers after a Summer shower. Not only that, but Vitamin P is free of charge and doubles in value when is given away!!! It is priceless and if it is used often enough can really boost young people's emotional health. How sad that a lack of it at home and in our schools leaves so many with a serious deficiency in self-esteem. How ironic then that praise is something that makes so many adults feel uncomfortable. So there's no need to go over the top with the compliments, just try slipping in little bits of praise where you can:

"You've done a great job of tidying up your room Chloe"
"Blimey Joe, my car has never looked so clean"...
"You've really tried hard with that maths homework tonight Josh"...

Try to resist the urge to do the Highland Fling every time a dirty dish is washed or a sock finds its way into the laundry basket though! Just acknowledge small steps in the right direction and you will soon see that praise works far better than criticism, whatever the person's age. And try letting young people overhear you praising them to other people, as that will really fluff up their feathers:
"You should see how tidy her room is now!" …
"He did a brilliant job of his Art project last week"…
As a bonus when you focus on the positives, this magically lift your own mood as well.

Vitamin P is definitely a powerful force in difficult situations, as the family I met in school one day were about to find out. They were really struggling with Joe, their thirteen year old and his younger brother Arron. Teachers, Social Workers and the Community Police Officer had all run out of ideas on how to deal with the boys' anti-social behaviour. Mum knew that they needed stronger boundaries at home and wondered if keeping them both in at night as a punishment was the answer. *"Has anyone tried using praise with Joe and Arron? Or rewarding them when they behave?"* I asked and the room went very quiet. I suggested that instead of taking things *away from* the boys (like seeing their friends after tea) that instead when they had a good day, they had an *extra* five minutes with their mates. A sea of sceptical faces gazed back at me, but Mum was keen to try my idea. The next time we all met in school, I could see that she was much happier.

Not only was Joe's behaviour 100% better, but she had tried the same approach with his younger brother Arron. He too had now started to do some of the housework, enticed with the idea of having an extra five minutes on his X Box. The Police Officer said that there was no longer any need for the boys to be on their radar and the school were happy with the improvements too - *and all down to Vitamin P.*

Praise is a great way to motivate younger children as well, and is a much easier way of getting them to do what you want them to do without too much resistance. My sister proved this theory when she took my niece Poppy to the weekly Mother and Toddler group. It was the usual mix of harassed mums and over-heated children, the little ones taking no notice whatsoever of their mums instructions. Apart from Poppy that is who ran straight back to her mum when she was called, for the hug that was waiting. One particular day, two of the other mums snorted behind her spitefully and one said *"Ooo, fancy saying 'thank you' to a child for coming back to you - how funny is that?!"* My sister felt hurt at first, but not for long. She realised that if they too had used praise instead of empty threats, their children might have been beautifully behaved as well.

Our society seems more and more focussed on 'outcomes' these days, rather than recognising the effort that has been put in to different things. The knock on effect is that young people's anxiety levels are off the scale as they struggle to please others.

Counselling services have ridiculously long waiting lists and many dedicated Head Teachers are being asked to see their students as percentage figures rather than the young people they really are. This is soul-destroying on both sides and student's confidence suffers when they feel they are 'under achieving'. Vitamin P would wonders with these students, especially those who struggle academically. They need to know that they can still be successful, despite not achieving good exam grades. *So we should all be motivating them instead of lowering their self-esteem.*

In reality, employers value other skills like reliability and enthusiasm just as much as they do exam results. Lots of people have done brilliantly in life despite having not done well at school. As a parent reassure your child that you love them and are proud of them *whatever* their results are. Encourage them to put their best effort in and to prepare well for tests of course, but help them to keep things in perspective. Remind them that learning goes on all through their lives and not just when they are at school.

How very different life is for those young people that you hear being talked about in the supermarket queue or on the playground: *"Oh, she is so shy / naughty / cheeky. Nothing like her brother was at that age. He was such a good boy"* and the poor thing is usually listening to the entire conversation! I remember a meeting in school I was invited to with a student, his mum and teacher.

I was mortified to hear his mum being told by the teacher that her son was *"pretty useless at reading"*. I could almost hear his self-esteem crashing to the floor, at the same time as my jaw. So I am eternally grateful for the fact that my parents have never once compared me with my two sisters or them to me. We've each been encouraged to use our own talents, whether that was my school gymnastics team, Lou doing well in exams or Babs making everyone laugh.

When I left College at eighteen, I found my confidence hitting rock bottom when I couldn't find a job for six *l-o-n-g* months. I remember walking around town in the rain wondering what on earth my future held. Do you know that even then, my parents still found things to praise me for? Yes, it might have only to say that I had done a good job of the washing up, but I knew they were on my side.

<u>SO</u>:

Praise the effort far more than any results &
Notice and praise even small improvements.

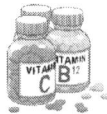

'Constructive criticism is about finding something good and positive to soften the blow of the real critique.'   *- Paula Abdul*

Chapter 3 - Considerate Criticism

Where Vitamin P builds confidence, criticism tears it down like a poison. It should carry a Government Health Warning, it is so destructive. And while adults can sift through criticism like prospectors panning for gold, young people find this really difficult to do. Some feel so afraid to put their efforts on the line that they don't even bother to try. Hurtful words can scar for a lifetime when we are young and there are definitely adults who take a grisly delight in humiliating young people. Perhaps they think that criticism will somehow improve their behaviour - but they are 100% wrong. *Criticism is never a motivator and used often enough, it utterly corrodes young personalities.*

My blood reached boiling point one day when our daughter came home from school looking utterly fed up. She said that her French teacher had embarrassed her in front of the whole class - again. Even though she had only been studying the language for six months, we thought she had grasped it really well and was enjoying it. But instead of being encouraging, her teacher had said loudly that her test results *"were okay, for her"*. Hardly surprising then that she gave up the subject as soon as she could.

I remember too one morning when I walked to work and heard a young apprentice being shouted at in the middle of the street. His boss was bawling *"No you twit, that isn't the way you do it!"* while the red faced young man looked down at his work boots uncomfortably. I only just about stopped myself from flying to his rescue like Wonder Woman to remind his boss that we <u>all</u> have to learn from our mistakes - just like he did at that age!

Perhaps even worse for young people's confidence are those oh-so-subtle criticisms. The disapproving look, the "tut" or raised eyebrow that brings the uneasy feeling of having 'messed up' in some way. Those tactics are a million miles away from constructive comments like *"You've got a much better school report this term Sarah and your English teacher says that your spelling is really good now! Perhaps I can help you to work on your Maths and Science if you're struggling with those?"* Try to look for progress not perfection and blend honesty with consideration. Be critical of an action or behaviour rather than of an entire personality, so *"That was a really lazy / selfish / nasty thing to do"* rather than *"You are such a lazy / selfish / nasty person."*

Over the years, our straight talking Dad has sat one or the other of us down for a Talk. Usually that has meant that he has seen *"a pattern evolving"* as he is in the habit of calling it and has felt duty bound to offer advice. These criticisms have come from his worry for us and we have taken them as best as we could.

By starting with a positive you will find it is accepted a lot more easily. *"You are such a caring type of person Joe, do you think sometimes other people take advantage of you?* Instead of saying something like *"Why are you such a doormat Joe, letting people walk all over you like that?!"*

Perhaps most importantly of all, remember that for many young people their own worst enemy is themselves. Their appearance, popularity and achievements all come under attack from their own critical eyes. Hearing them say that they are "ugly", "stupid" or "fat" is heart-breaking for the people around them. So instead of telling them to *"stop being stupid"*, take the time to listen to their insecurities and help them to feel more positive. Rather than comparing themselves to air-brushed TV celebrities.

SO:

Make a praise sandwich to make criticism easier to swallow.

Chapter 4: Respectfully Yours

Respect – that rare and special quality not usually associated with the young, thanks to the Media. They don't write about the bravery that some young people show every day in coping with really tough lives. Like the peroxide blond Tiffany, whose rebellious eyes weighed me up one afternoon in school. She was something of a legend in the Staff Room was Tiffany and as she told me her story, my trepidation turned to respect. She explained that when she was in Primary School, she had come home one afternoon to find her Mum had collapsed on the floor. She had taken an overdose, just as her dad had done the year before. Tiffany now lived with her Nan opposite the cemetery where both her parents were buried. As I looked at her eyes swimming in rivers of black eyeliner, I felt too upset to say anything for a while. No wonder her behaviour in school was so out of control I thought. *It was amazing she managed to turn up at all.*

Then sometimes the most unlikely students can earn your respect. Like Shane, the notorious Bad Boy in Year 11 whose reputation was well known. I was expecting someone very different from the thin young man who stood examining the floor in front of me when we first met. He admitted that he *'hated school'* and *"didn't understand most of his lessons"*. The problem seemed to be that he needed to wear glasses but like lots of the lads, he wouldn't. So he couldn't actually read the whiteboard in class and had got more and more behind with his work.

He seemed so dejected that I said I would take him to visit the local college the week after to look at the mechanics courses there. I knew there was no way he would go on his own, but as we walked to my car on the appointed day Shane suddenly strode on ahead without me. I started to wonder if the teachers had been right about him, so imagine my surprise as I saw him standing by my car - waiting to hold the door open for me! But that isn't the type of story that sells newspapers does it? It's so much better for sales figures to write about yet another 'wild teen' who has knocked over an old lady on a Zebra Crossing and stolen her disability scooter.

And how could I forget Charlotte, who must have been around thirteen when I met her in school. She had been born with such a badly disfigured face that she had already endured far too many operations. No surprise that she was badly bullied in school, so I assumed that her self-esteem would be non-existent. But as we talked about her plans for the future, I realized how wrong I was. Not only did she volunteer at the local Children's Hospice, she also took care of her disabled mum and younger brother. She didn't seem to have the tiniest bit of self-pity and told me with quiet conviction that she *"planned to be a Nurse one day and make a difference"*. I have no doubt at all that Charlotte is doing just that today.

Looking back I have found that those adults who had faith in me made a *huge* difference to my confidence.

When I was 10 yrs old, I had the happiest year of my school life at Saltway Middle School. With its Victorian arched windows and red tiled floors, I can still hear our Head Teacher's important shoes echoing down the corridors. Mr Watts had an air of royalty about him which managed to blend kindness and fairness perfectly. He expected us to treat each other in the same way and it didn't matter at all that we were *"just kids"*, as he talked to us in the same way he would to another adult. Miss Roberts our R.E teacher was just the same, with her patient grey eyes, she never once raised her voice in the four years she taught me. And she had every reason to at times believe me! I remember one afternoon when she asked me to read the note I had just passed to the young man sitting in front of me to the whole class. With my cheeks burning defiantly I refused, and the whole class held their breath. After what seemed like an eternity, Miss Roberts asked me to throw the guilty note in the bin and her disappointment filled the room. There was no shouting, only tiredness in her gaze as I vowed inwardly to do well in my R.E exam. Years later she told me that had been her plan all along.

Another teacher I really admired was the maths teacher at Eden Technology College. One morning I could hear his soft Welsh voice saying to a student *"Marcus are you tired this morning or have you missed your breakfast again?"*

"No? Well do you think you could <u>try</u> to stay awake in my maths lesson then please?" he said man-to-almost-man. Later the same day I could hear him talking to another class who were slowly poaching in a hot classroom *"Whew, it is really warm in here isn't it? Why don't we start by opening the windows a bit wider and drinking some water?"* Nothing so incredible about that you might think, unless you had overheard the teacher before him shouting at his class *"Ok you lot - wake up, shut up and READ."* He had obviously not heard the advice of the American teacher Rita Pierson who said *"Kids don't learn from teachers they don't like"*.

If only my spiteful Junior School teacher Miss Ratcliff had taken that advice to heart. A pasty faced woman with huge glasses and greasy hair, she seemed to delight in scaring our class half to death. I remember the day she embarrassed me to the soles of my school shoes by shouting *"Now children, shall we all stop and give Ellen time to catch up, as she is <u>so</u> far behind"*. No wonder I have never liked Maths from that day to this - and I was only eight years old! Yes, it is true that some young people have *far* too much to say for themselves, but that doesn't mean we should stop showing them respect and expecting the same in return. Psychologists call this 'unconditional regard' and revolves around listening to other people's ideas with an open mind. And when I met Tom one cold November morning in school, I found out how this really does work.

He talked earnestly about his determination to carry on with his Jehovah's Witness preaching when he left school by *"buying a Doughnut Van"* to fund his Ministry'. I was speechless for a minute as I found myself wrestling with the strange image of Tom simultaneously feeding hungry souls and stomachs. Until that is, he explained how he planned to apply to the Princes Trust for a Business Start-Up Loan when he was old enough. Suddenly I could see it all actually working for him and felt mortified to think of what might have happened if I had laughed at his idea. *What would that have done for his confidence?*

Then there was Charlie, who told me that he had been watching a tribute to the reptile expert Steve Irwin on TV the night before. He said in a matter of fact way that he too wanted to *"milk snakes"* like his hero, the job involving removing their venom to be used in the cosmetics industry. I found myself biting my lip again to stop a smile, before somehow managing to ask Charlie how he hoped to earn a living milking snakes in the North of England? He explained that he was in fact saving up to go to Australia, and however unlikely his plan seemed to be, who was I to judge? Instead I suggested that he develop a "back-up plan" in case his snake milking dream didn't come true.

Respect as a concept has come a long way in the last decade. Whether we are at work, in hospital or on holiday, everyone seems desperate for our opinions and our feedback.

There are customer care policies displayed proudly in doctor's surgeries, hotels and reception areas assuring us of how very important we are. Apart from in our High Schools it seems, where there is no shortage of reminders about what is expected of students;
'Wear the right uniform..
Turn up to lessons on time..
Complete all homework..
Walk calmly around school'...

It has always seemed so one sided to me though and I am convinced that it would make an amazing difference to student's morale if they were asked to write their own Students Charter (*see page 64). This would reflect the things that students felt were important to their time in education. They would be reassured that their ideas would being taken seriously and that any targets they had were achievable. *Target grades would be agreed with students rather than calculated from the SATS tests they took at the end of Year 6 when they were only 11yrs old. I know as a mother and professional that when these predicted grades are too high, instead of motivating students, they cause SO much stress instead.*

If you think about it in another way. Can you imagine joining Slimming World and your group leader informed you how much weight you were expected to lose over the coming week? The next time you *went to a meeting you were made to feel like a Total* Failure because you hadn't achieved the target they had set for you? There would be a public outcry and Slimming World would we sued!

So why is this allowed to happen in our High Schools? And why are our so many of our dedicated teachers and students under ridiculous pressure to achieve these fanciful results? It is a 'No-Win' situation on both sides.

When Kevin Courtney, the General Secretary of the National Union of Teachers spoke at their annual conference in April 2018, he hit home with some incredibly worrying facts. He said that *"Our country has some of the most unhappy children in the developed world. They are more anxious about tests than any other country and school is now cited as the main cause of stress for 65% of 12-year olds and 82% of 16 year olds."*

Thank goodness then that there are those schools that are <u>so</u> skilled in motivating students, that it is a pleasure to work there. From the moment you arrive in the morning there is a warm welcome and the feeling that students and teachers respect one another. Both hold doors open for each other and relaxing music drifts up from the Dining Hall along with the smell of freshly baked shortbread being cooked for break time. Staff swap jokes with students and there is a real feeling that *"we are all in this together".*

Compare that to other schools where a depressing fog seems to hang in the corridors and staff and students are constantly criticised. Morale is so low that staff are counting the days until they can retire, even the young ones. How can anyone hope to learn in such an environment?

It should be no surprise then that attendance is a huge problem in these schools, as one teacher explained:-

"If we don't want to be in school, how can we expect students to feel any differently?" It certainly makes you wonder what happened to having a childhood and learning being FUN. It is <u>so</u> sad that teaching is no longer the rewarding and respected profession it once was and that some school staff can't help but let their negativity spill over to students. Surely if young people miss out on what should be a carefree time in their lives, they are much more likely to suffer from with anxiety and depression later on? Which is why the Government is now committing over a billion pounds to train more professionals to tackle this.

As parents we can make our feelings known to the school Governors whose job it is to support our children and good schools will welcome our questions and take them seriously. When Ofsted inspects schools now, they look at how they involve parents, so remind them of this if you don't feel you are being listened to. Tell them about the effects that too much pressure is having on your child and insist on more emotional support for those who need it.

SO: *Show respect to receive it & Welcome ideas with an open mind.*

'Attitudes are more important than facts.'
– Dr Norman Vincent Peale

Chapter 5: Positive Thinking

We as adults know only too well that life isn't anything like a Disney film. Sadly we don't skip hand in hand down a yellow brick road. In fact the grown up world can be downright depressing at times with its money worries, job insecurities and all the countless other things we have no control over. Add to that all those issues that keep us awake at night, wondering how we are ever going to save the environment, exhausted donkeys and hungry polar bears. And while each of us *can* make a difference in the wider world, the only thing we really have complete control over are our own thoughts. So if we fill our minds with thoughts like these, our self-esteem soon disappears:-

" *No-one likes me"..*

"I am useless / ugly / fat"..

"Everyone is talking about me".

Those bleak 6 o'clock Headlines don't help to lift our mood either do they? So it is no surprise that young people can soon start to wonder how on earth they are ever going to survive in such a crazy world. They feel about as unprepared as a mountaineer in flip-flops. We three sisters were *so* lucky to have been given our own First Aid Kit by our wise parents. It has saved our emotional health many times over the years.

The pages of my copy have long since faded around the edges and the pages worn loose, but *The Power of Positive Thinking* by Dr Norman Vincent Peale is as relevant today as when it was written in the 1950's.

If by some chance Alex had read it, he probably wouldn't have been swallowing the paracetamols he was when he arrived in the Careers Office one Friday afternoon. The minute he sat down, all his negativity and self-doubt came pouring out:-

'There is no way I am ever going to get a job'..

'No employer will want to me with my rubbish 'A' level results'…

'I failed my Math GCSE <u>again</u> – what an idiot I am ...'
'Why do I bother.. Everyone thinks I'm a complete loser anyway'.

It wasn't long before the temperature in the room plummeted and even Alex had to admit that his gloomy thoughts weren't helping anyone. He agreed that he needed to change his negative thinking if he was ever going to find a job. So slowly and painfully over the following week we worked on this aspect and when I rang him later in the week he told me he had seen an apprenticeship which he wanted to apply for. When he called in to see me later that day, I noticed a change in him straight away. He looked much taller, standing straight instead of slouching, and I couldn't be sure but I think he had even brushed his hair. For the next hour we worked on his interview skills and I encouraged him to *imagine* feeling confident during the interview.

The next day he phoned me to say that he had been offered the job, even though he hadn't really got the experience that the company had been looking for. They had been "*bowled over*" by his enthusiasm, proof indeed of Dr Peale's words- *'Enthusiasm over rides everything'*.

Alex's experience reminded me of when our daughter was a toddler and had set herself the challenge of jumping off the back step, as children love to at that age. Although it was only a few inches off the ground, I can see her little face framed in curls and full of determination as she said "*I can do this, I know I can*". Of course she was over the moon when she did, and then spent the rest of the morning perfecting her new skill. A positive thinker at only three years old!

When I meet students in school who are struggling to feel positive, I ask them to complete one their own Dream Cloud. This is the outline of a cloud, where I ask them to write their hopes and dreams for the future. They find that taking a short break from their gloomy thoughts is like a holiday in itself. I encourage them to put their completed Cloud where they can see it at home every day so that it dissolves into their subconscious.

Sometimes even the smallest words can be the most powerful ones, as one inspiring Primary Head Teacher has discovered. He encourages his staff to add the tiny word YET at the end of sentences, to turn them into positive statements. The word has gradually changed the whole mood of his school and this is how it works in practise.

*"I can't read that word - **yet**…"*

*"I don't understand decimals – **yet**…"*

*"I haven't made any new friends – **yet**…"*

It works just as well with adults too:

*"I haven't lost any weight – **yet** …"*

*"I haven't stopped smoking – **yet** …"*

*"I haven't met Mr or Mrs Right – **yet**..*

What a pity that James' Maths teacher didn't use this magic word at all. She had just upset his whole class by telling them that *"without a C grade in their Maths exam, they would <u>never</u> get a good job"*. Little wonder that James had reacted badly, knowing full well that he hadn't a hope of doing well in any of his exams. He was not a strong student academically and had no good role models at home, living with his unemployed Dad who drank his days away. He was so worried about *"failing his exams"* that he was hardly sleeping and had even started to self-harm. His aggression in school was really an attempt to hide his crumbling confidence, thanks in no small part to Miss Thomas. Thankfully there was a happy ending for James just around the corner. When he left school he found an employer who saw his potential and offered him a job as a trainee mechanic.

Which is why we *all* need to reassure young people that they add up to so much more than grades on an exam paper! There are countless measures of success and high exam results don't automatically equal happy adults.

The charismatic TV chef Jamie Oliver would be the first to admit that his finest hour was most definitely *not* in the classroom. Being dyslexic, he found studying a real challenge and discovered that his real talents lay in the kitchen. He used his handicap with words to become a successful celebrity chef. Ethan too had overcome huge obstacles in his young life, having being born severely handicapped and needing 24 hour care. His determined mum wanted him to stay in mainstream education rather than go to a Special School, so he and his support worker Mike were a familiar sight in school steering his wheelchair through the crowds. When I first met him, Ethan told me that he wanted to be a sports coach when he left school, not mentioning his handicap at all. He seemed *so* much more positive than many of his able bodied friends and his physical disabilities had not crippled his ambitions. I was not at all surprised to hear then that Ethan did well in his exams and went on to the College of his choice.

Everyone feels negative and doubts themselves at times, adults being no exception. For me, the year I spent working in a Catholic 6th Form College was not a happy one, thanks to one sour faced teacher. It was only by giving myself a rousing Pep Talk every morning that I persuaded myself to go in to school at all some days. The mystified Caretaker often looked at me oddly as I sat in my car talking to myself, trying to pull myself together.
I refused to be bullied by Mrs Bailey, whose frosty attitude didn't change towards me at all. She eventually hung up her broomstick and retired.

Life inevitably life throws obstacles in our path that dull our joie de vivre. When I was twenty, my usual optimism deserted me after foolishly going camping in April. It was still *far* too cold to be sleeping outdoors and when I woke up on the second day, I was in so much pain with my right shoulder that we had to go home. The doctor referred me to one of many specialists who only seemed to make the pain worse. So I was beginning to resign myself to being that way for the rest of my life when I heard about an ex Red Beret turned physiotherapist named Mick Gillman. A 'tough old boot' in the nicest possible way, who at seventy four years of age had the physique of someone half his age.

I remember pulling up for the first time outside his modest terraced house in Crewe, watching a calf limping along the street being led by Mick. We watched open mouthed as he knelt down by the little animal and gave the bent leg a gentle tug. The calf gave itself a little shake and skipped off down the road - *completely healed.* Mick's treatment room was a testament to his skills with photos of well-known celebrities adorning the walls. So for the next six months he taught me exercises that would gradually restore my health and my confidence. More importantly, he showed me how to train my thoughts in true Army style. He drummed in to me that I had to first *imagine* myself being healthy again. So while I exercised on the hour every hour, I would visualise myself cycling down a country lane completely free of pain, the smell of Summer filling my nostrils.

Mick assured me that "*your body can only achieve what your mind believes it can*" and explained that if athletes are full of negativity they can't train effectively. Slowly and painfully over the months that followed, my shoulder and my confidence improved until the day came when I didn't need to visit Mick any more. But I have never forgotten him. He taught me that your mind is your body's strongest muscle. He proved to me that to achieve yours goals, you first need to train your mind.

'Do not follow where the path may lead…
Go instead where there is no path and make a trail.'
-Ralph Waldo Emerson

Chapter 6: Becoming an Individual

Have you ever been hit by a revolving door? I have and it hurt. Well that is exactly how so many parents feel as their children morph into adulthood. No wonder they can feel totally bewildered as their offspring seem to change overnight. Where is the sweet child who brought you wild flowers home as a gift or trapped beetles in a jar especially for you? Parents feel such an icy draft as their children pull away in a bid to find out *'who they are'*. It feels exactly like unrequited love but this distancing is a natural part of growing up. We parents feel totally rejected as they swing precariously from carefree child to grumpy teenager in the space of minutes. Lego bricks are exchanged for hair gel and looks of contempt.

All of a sudden, their demands and opinions seem to be part of everything, so it's little wonder that exhausted parents struggle to keep control. But understanding that all the stroppiness is more about them flexing their Independence Muscle, can really help.

Try hard not to make them feel guilty by saying wistfully *"how much they have changed"* - even if it is true. Letting go can be a real challenge, as one mum was discovering at the Bridgewater Pottery Centre we visited in Stoke-on-Trent last year. We had a brilliant afternoon admiring the hand painted ceramics there and were just queuing to pay, when I tuned in to the conversation behind me. A boy of about seven was decorating the mug he had made at a table with a group of other children, while his mum watched like a hawk:-

Mum – *"Why don't you stick the handle on to your mug before you paint your design on Harry?"*

Harry – *"Because the handle will be in my way then Mum and it'll be harder to paint around it ..."*

Mum - *"Well (loud sigh) you're making a right mess of it – look at your brothers mug, it's so neatly painted! Here let me show you"* (*as she grabbed his paint brush*) Harry (upset) – *"I want to do it myself Mum - it's my Birthday, not yours!"*

Poor lad just wanted to do something by himself but his mum obviously couldn't let go. It reminded me of the middle aged brother and sister who lived together near me in Crewe. Their elderly mother hadn't allowed them to do *anything* for themselves as they grew up, so they had no friends or ever socialised. The three of them lived in a dark Victorian house, prisoners of her fears and chained to the house like they were in a Dickens novel.

When they do feel secure, children can develop a real sense of who they are and not care quite so much about what other people think of them. So rather than spending their lives trying to 'fit in', they feel proud of their uniqueness. As the actor and comedian Robin Williams said: *'We are all given a little spark of madness; make sure you don't lose yours.'*

An adult that young people grow to respect can make all the difference in their lives, and my Mums happiest memory of her school years was in Mr Machin's class. He was the one who convinced his 'shy' pupil to audition for the leading role in the school play and it was he who gave her the courage to accept the challenge. Not only was the play a huge success but his confidence in her helped to shape Mum's own future teaching career. *Mr Machin has never been forgotten, even after all this time.*

In just the same way, the children at my sisters' school will definitely remember her. She is such a breath of fresh air that her little protégés devour everything she teaches them with relish and learning is so much FUN when she is in the classroom. Her bubbly personality makes each pupil feel important and she celebrates each of their achievements with bright stickers or a 'dip' in her Treats Chest filled with little prizes. Being such a strong character herself goes a long way towards her pupils feeling good about themselves. *Which is even more amazing because they are all Autistic.*

Learning to have more confidence in our opinions was the idea behind the Family Meetings we held at home as we were growing up. They started off as a way of 'airing our grievances' I think, which there were plenty of in a house with four women in it. Once a month we took it in civilized turns to share our injustices, worries and ideas while poor Dad refereed. We were never patronized and there were relatively few tantrums, even from Dad! We learned to see each other's point of view eventually and to appreciate that things are rarely black and white.

Helping young people to get the balance right between expressing themselves and being part of our straight-laced society is not easy. Yes, there are those fashion icons who ooze self-confidence and individuality, but most of us find we need to edit our personalities for the outside world. Letting their individuality shine through is vital for young people though, so encourage it to flourish. And meeting a blend of different people is a great way to stretch their horizons. Few things do this better than voluntary work and while the concept of giving up their time *"for free"* is one they struggle with, they start to appreciate why it is so valuable. They also discover talents and interests they didn't even know they had. It was noble Queen Victoria who said:-

'I do not worry what others think of me, as it is far more important what I think of them.'

So:

Let go of the reins and give young people enough room to grow.

Encourage new experiences that will shape their personalities.

'A peacefulness follows any decision – even the wrong one.'

- Rita Mae Brown

Chapter 7: Confident Decisions

Decisions being such a normal part of life, you would think we would be experts in making them wouldn't you? So why do they bring <u>so</u> much stress with them? Whether it is little ones like what to have for tea, or huge ones like whether to start a family, they all have an impact on our life. Many struggle with making those elusive 'right' choices so much that they wobble on the edge of uncertainty for years, hoping that they will somehow *"know for sure"* one day. Yet young people are expected to know how to make decisions about their future when they are only fifteen! At that age you would have found me hanging round the local Chip Shop with my friends and a smuggled bottle of cider, not grappling with Life's Mysteries.

Back then I had the same priorities my friends had.
Boys, music and what to wear to the school disco on Friday. Add to that the fact that teenagers haven't yet developed the emotional or psychological tools they need to see too far ahead. So the more pressure we put on them, the less they can think clearly. Lots of adults don't share this point of view at all though, like the Head Teacher I once met who informed me that in his opinion, *"all eleven year olds should have a clear career plan"*.

As I stared at him in disbelief all I could wonder was why anyone would put that kind of pressure on a child? The proverbial question of *"what do you want to do when you grow up / leave school?"* is the dread of many young people, most who have no idea at all. And why on earth should they have? You can't 'put an old head on young shoulders' and at fifteen, young people are only at the start of a very long journey. Parents can help younger children to prepare for the bigger decisions later in life by letting them make lots of little ones. So instead of doing everything for them, try to step back and give them chance to figure things out for themselves. True, it might only be which clothes to wear or what to have for lunch, but each decision lays down a thin layer of confidence. Help them to understand that their choices have consequences too.

The fascinating thing about decisions is that we all approach them in different ways. Some jump in before they have barely had time to think, while others miss out because they think things over for way too long. Just like turning up at the end of a Car Boot Sale and finding all the bargains have gone. Leaving decisions to the last minute usually means making them with lots of stress.

And Jodie had done just that it seemed when she came in to the Careers Office one Friday afternoon. *"I haven't applied to college yet…"* she said blushing *"Could you phone them for me and see which courses they've got left?"* She explained that she had felt so nervous about getting her decision 'wrong', that she had put it off all Summer.

Then there are those young people who seem to have such a casual approach to decisions that it is almost scary to watch. This group are usually prone to following the crowd, a technique which relinquishes all responsibility should things go wrong. It is a perfect technique for those who don't trust their own judgement, as they simply copy what their brother, sister or friends choose without thinking what is right for them.

But that type of decision making rarely leads to a happy ending, just as Max was finding out. He had come to see me for advice on applying to University - the day before the deadline! He told me that because his friend was going to Bangor University, he was thinking of applying there as well. But it was soon clear though that Max didn't even realise that Bangor was in Wales! Trying to follow his thought process was like watching a trapeze artist fly from one high bar to another without a net. And if anyone knew about making wobbly decisions at the same age, it was me. The Summer I left school was spent in the local library trying to digest the entire Careers Section. I had no idea what I was hoping to find, as I looked in vain for the Job of My Dreams, but I had to start somewhere. My ideas at the time ranged from working in a Garden Centre because I liked being outside and Journalism because I was good at English. So I wrote to every newspaper Editor in the city asking for an interview and sat back to wait for the offers to flood in. What a shock I had when only <u>one</u> newspaper replied, but the Editor of the Leek Post & Times must have seen something in my letter and offered to meet me.

I can still remember his blue eyes twinkling, as he realised I knew nothing about the real job at all. Of course, if I'd followed my Dad's favourite bit of advice about making decisions, I might of fared better. He advises *"getting all the facts together first to see the overall picture"*. Usually he says, there is a theme, a pattern or a common thread. The Professor of Science I heard being interviewed as I drove home one evening said this was exactly the same technique he uses himself too. He explained that he tackles life's important decisions in a *'methodical way'* and looks at the *'probability'* of one outcome being more successful than another. Using this type of thinking he breaks down decisions in the same way that he would a scientific experiment. He keeps emotions out of the equation.

Sound advice indeed, with the only problem being that from a young person's point of view, all this takes far too much time. It is so much easier to just ask someone else what to do, or make decisions without thinking too much about them. The fact is, weighing up choices is hard work and lots of young people just don't want to spend time wrestling with them. Many would much rather accept a total stranger's point of view than torture themselves with complicated decisions - and it is that which makes them so vulnerable.

'If you look for too long - you may never leap at all' ...
said Dr Howard Fuller the American Civil Rights
activist. So when enough time has been spent gathering
the facts, the next natural step needs to be action and that
is the sticking point for lots of young people. Even if it is
only taking one small step, this last part of the decision
making process is vital. The trouble is, when we lack
confidence this last bit can be HUGE. They hover on the
edge of a decision and then just when they are about to
take the plunge, they fall back into the tumble drier of
indecision all over again.

So if you know someone who is struggling to make a
decision, try to gently nudge them in the right direction
like a mother bird moving her little ones to the edge of
the nest. Remember though that like barnacles clinging
to a rock, young people won't let go of a bad decision
unless they have a Safety Net. That's why it is so
important to let them know that you are there to catch
them if they fall, which will then give them the
confidence they need to jump.

'He who never made a mistake, never made a discovery.'

- Samuel Smiles

'Tread softly, because you tread on my dreams.'
- Wilfred Owen

Chapter 8-Handling Disappointments

Life seems like one big Amusement Arcade at times doesn't it? One day we win, the next we lose and we do our best to take things in our stride. But while adults are more philosophical, young peoples' confidence can be knocked completely out of shape by disappointments. So can we prepare them in some way and spare them the agony of heartbreak? Or would that just give them a false sense of security? I remember a Christmas party when I was little where our teacher had kindly made sure that there were chairs for everyone for our game of Musical Chairs. We skipped round and round for what seemed like hours until we collapsed in a heap, totally exhausted! No-one won and no-one lost, but it was the most boring game ever!

The Head Teacher was such a lovely man too and announced at the end of the Sports Day that *"There are no losers at Highfields Primary School today"*. He then proceeded to give out a whole handful of rosettes to each Team Captain, one for each child!

But far from being pleased, the crowd felt angry and confused. They wanted winners to cheer and felt cheated. A nice idea in theory, but surely learning how to lose graciously is teaching an important life lesson too? Trying to insulate young people against disappointments will only make life harder for them in the future after all. With experience, their resilience will grow and they will learn to bounce back.

The last year of High School needs *lots* of resilience as students prepare for exams and leaving school after eleven years. They often feel in desperate need of confidence when they realise that having looked forward to huge salaries and exciting careers they are instead on minimum pay and the first rung of the ladder. '*The world might well be their oyster*' as the saying goes, but they will need to open plenty of empty shells over the years until they find one! Not everyone is destined for fame, fortune and happily-ever-afters. Some parents seem to react much worse than their children when faced with disappointments. The agony of them losing a football match or not being invited to a sleepover can be almost too much to bear. So they go to any lengths to make things better and say childish things like '*I can't believe they didn't pick you for the school play again – it is so unfair*''. Perhaps this is why some young people grow up thinking that the world is 'against them' when things don't go their way?

It can certainly be a balancing act trying not to be dismissive of disappointments and at the same time not making too much of them. Impatient remarks like *"Well it isn't the end of the world"* can really sting when young people are upset. So much more helpful to just let them talk things through and genuinely acknowledge their hurt. Young people do have a tendency to replay the catalogue of their failures when they feel low, so remind them that *everyone* makes mistakes. Tell them about some of the things that you have got wrong in your own life to cheer them up. *That should take quite a while if you are anything like me.* Remember that disastrous job interview or the time you dropped the baton on Sports Day? The more philosophical you can be about your own disappointments, the more young people will learn to take them in their stride.

One disappointment I will never forget happened when I was sixteen, on holiday in the Isle of Wight. I fell head over heels for a young man from Derby named Chris. He was there under sufferance like me with his family, so our holiday romance blossomed like summer roses. And when we got home, we spoke on the phone every day and planned for me to catch the train to see him the following weekend. I can still feel the tingle of excitement as the train pulled away from the platform in Stoke and we had a brilliant weekend. Chris agreed a return trip the following weekend and I hardly slept all week with excitement.

I kept myself busy after school doing housework, to the amusement of my parents. The whole family entered into the spirit of things with my Dad even painting the garage doors in his honour. So imagine how I felt on the Friday night before his arrival when the phone rang and it was Chris pretending to be "too ill" to come over the next day. I was devastated and reduced to a tear-stained heap for three whole days. I lay in my darkened room crying to every sad song on the radio, nursing my broken heart. But eventually when I had no tears left to cry, I headed for the kitchen - my heartbreak had left me starving hungry. He was the first of many ill-fated teenage crushes and I marvel now looking back, that the magazines I read at the time never so much as mentioned being let down. Perhaps if they had, I might have been a bit more prepared for them!

So: - *Keep expectations realistic, so that disappointments are kept in perspective.*

DETOUR

'Say what you mean and mean what you say.'
- Dr Patty Tublin

Chapter 9: Secure Boundaries

Have you ever tried to grow sweet peas? I have and without the bamboo canes to hold them securely, they just flopped and got all tangled up. It is the same for young people. They need a strong structure to grow in the right direction. So when a "no" becomes a "yes" too often they soon get confused. So when the rules of the game keep changing, chaos inevitably follows. Can you imagine if one morning as you drove to work, the Highway Code had completely changed and everyone was doing their own thing? It wouldn't be long before you were too stressed and confused to drive anywhere would it? *That's because we all need to be clear what the rules are and exactly how far they can be stretched.*

The trouble is, if you are a soft-hearted parent like me, it can be a real struggle at times to say the "no" that needs to be said. So remind yourself of the devoted boyfriend or girlfriend who let you get away with murder and walk all over them. How they *really* started to annoy you after a while! Well that's exactly how young people feel when they have a parent who they know they can manipulate. Without boundaries, they soon start to feel that no-one cares what they do, so it is little wonder that their behaviour spirals out of control.

Troy was certainly heading in that direction when I met him in school, as no sooner had he sat down than he dug out a tattered newspaper clipping from his pocket to show me. The headline read '*Teen in Local Shop Robbery*' and had a photo of him in the bottom corner. As he looked at me expectantly I realised that this was Troy's 'claim to fame' and the sum of his achievements to date. It was almost as if he felt proud of being "*the worst student ever*" as he put it - how desperately sad was that? Caitlin too was well known for her boundary-stretching escapades, as this conversation I overheard shows:

"*Caty, you know you are not allowed to bring those energy drinks in here...*"

"*Why not?*"

"*Because that is one of the College rules...*"

"*Well it's a stupid rule and I am not throwing my drink away...*"

"*Okay then I'll have to send you home if you won't respect our rules...*"

"*Go on then, see if I care...*" So home she went, but the next day I noticed that she had bought a bottle of fruit juice in to College instead. Caty too was gradually learning that if you want to get on well in life, you have to follow rules. The truth is that if we don't teach children to respect boundaries from the start, we are only setting them up for a huge shock later. In the real world Caitlin would have been sent home by her boss and told not to bother coming back.

My younger sister has worked with Primary School children for over thirty years and is as devoted to them as they are to her. Some are <u>very</u> attention seeking and have a real talent for soaking up the limelight. She uses the phrase *"any attention is good attention"* to describe how they try every trick available to steal the spotlight.

To protect your own sanity, young people need to be completely clear about what is expected of them. So if you expect them to wash up after tea and it is still there at nine o'clock, calmly tell them that they will be getting their own tea next time. There's no need to sound like an Army Officer barking out instructions from morning to night though: *"Stop doing that..."* *"Sit down ..."* *"Stand still..."* *"Eat your peas."* Young people don't need a choke-chain around their necks which you pull every time they step out of line. What a miserable way of living for both of you that would be.

I have found that it isn't possible to change someone else's behaviour by nagging them to death. Yes they'll go along with your demands for a while, but they'll find other ways to rebel. So in the long run it is much easier if you can both just sit down and talk instead. When you try to hide your emotions under a veneer of being in control, you will probably over-react and say things you can't stick to anyway. Better to wait until you have both calmed down before giving out harsh punishments which you will only regret. *You really will look like you don't know what you're doing then.*

Simply acknowledge any tears of regret without wobbling, even if an apology comes in later. Beware of an ambush if your boundaries are not strong enough, as like an advancing Army, shrewd young people will trample you under foot. Instead do your best to rise above the rapids instead of behaving like a teen yourself. You should be the one to suggest a 'cool down' as no-one *really* wins an argument and angry words can't be taken back once said. Much better to pick your battles rather than moaning about every discarded crisp packet or pile of clothes. Stay calm and respectful when you want things done, with sentence starters like: *"Could you...?"* or *"Would you mind...?"* Younger children respond far better to games than instructions anyway: *"Let's see who can tidy their toys away fastest shall we!?"* *"I wonder who will do the best job of washing the dishes tonight!?"* And if you handle these smaller feuds, then they hopefully won't escalate.

Accepting that young people have different priorities will also help when it comes to turning a blind eye to the biscuit crumbs on the sofa. It is amazing how when you use a sense of humour, you earn more co-operation as well. When I ventured in to our daughter's room one day, the sight that met my eyes almost took my breath away. There were mounds of clothes strewn everywhere, used makeup wipes and cotton wool buds all over the floor - even the cat on the bed had put his paws over his eyes!

So when she got in from school, I casually remarked; *"Bad news love, your room had been burgled and the thieves have turned it upside down!!!"* We both laughed, but she got the message and tidied up. Like skilled magicians, some young people can weave an argument that is so complicated, you find yourself agreeing to all sorts of things without even realising it though:

"Mum, can I borrow some money for a new eyeliner 'cos this one has run out?"

"Run out? But you only bought it at the weekend!"

"No it was last weekend mum and it was a 2-4-1 deal anyway"

"Hmm and you had the eyeliner as part of the deal?"

"Yes so it was only half price really"

"Well y-e-s, but it was only the other day – what on earth are you doing with the stuff!"

"So if it was half price, so that means you owe me £2.50 and I can buy another one then"

"But...hold on, I gave you the money in the first place"

"Ah, thanks mum" (said with a winning smile)

"Now hang on a minute ..."

Beware that if you let the Rules slide too often, even the fairest of young people will take you for granted, as I know only too well! That doesn't mean that they are on the Slippery Slope, they just want to see how much they could get away with. These are the very times that set the tone for the future, so be on your guard. Make an extra effort or the rules will get stretched out of all proportion.

Young people who have only ever been kept on a sunny window sill will be devastated by the first real frost, especially if they have been led to believe they are invincible. How many meetings have I sat in at school where everyone present suggested a hundred different ways of helping a student in trouble - while they just sat there? Elaborate support plans were hatched and I found myself wondering at what point the young person in question might perhaps take *some* responsibility for their own actions?

Of course, setting boundaries does inevitably lead to friction, but arguing rarely changes the other person's point of view. Far easier to accept that you won't agree on everything, and try to listen to each other instead. Making sure that you keep the lines of communication open means that they will still confide in you when it really matters. If communications really do break down for a while and the boundaries that you have so carefully put in place have been trampled on, it is such a relief to sit down and admit that you feel completely fed up. Remember that showing your own emotions is not a sign of weakness...

So: *Be consistent - Negotiate where you can, but try and remember who is in charge!*

'To be yourself in a world that is constantly trying to make you something else, is the greatest accomplishment.'
        -Ralph Waldo Emerson

Pulling It All Together

I have to admit that there have been some lengthy pauses in writing my book. There have also been times when I have felt desperately in need of advice myself. I have wondered how on earth I have managed to spend all these years working with young people and being a Mum and yet still have so much to learn. I have learned so much in writing it, and that is how I know my advice works! Parenting is a lot like putting together a healthy meal. You use all the ingredients that you *think* are the right ones and then adapt them as you go along. It is a complex recipe and we all wish we understood our children more.

'Just be Yourself' is I hope relevant to any adult who works with young people, as they too have a key role to play in building their self-esteem.

And you will have noticed that I am passionate about doing what I can do to change the ridiculously pressurized exam culture that we seem to have adopted in this country. My book is a plea to the people who develop these policies to nurture our young people instead of stretching them to breaking point. I am personally working towards a time when students are *consulted with* rather than given their exam target grades. While individuals can't change the entire education system it is true, as parents and teachers we should always be questioning the things which affect our children and students.

Many dedicated teachers and managers are powerless to do more for their students because of their own job constraints and that has to be wrong. They are relying on parents to press for change, so speak up at Parents Evenings and ask questions. Insist that young people are not weighed down with revision, exams and stress. Politely inform those people with influence know that your child *needs a balanced life* and time to enjoy their childhood. That way, they can take the time they need to learn how to **Just Be Themselves.**

Acknowledgements

Thank you to my own Amazing Parents for setting such an awe inspiring example and for being proud of me when I needed it most. I have spent a long time looking forward to presenting you with the first copy of my book. Thank you to our daughter Maisie who has made us so proud for the past sixteen years. She is growing in to a mature and beautiful young lady. To my best friends in all the world; my sisters Babs and Lou. Thank you for your love and support, the scaffolding in my life. To my amazing Aunties Joyce and Nance and Uncles Norm and Roy, for sharing your ageless wisdom with me.

And to my lovely friends Julie, Jan, Elaine and Sue who have raised seven confident young people between them. They know a thing or two about being great parents. To my great friends Di & Bri, who always seem to be planning their next adventure. *Thank you to Bri especially for proof reading my book* and to Nick for all your patience in the past.

A huge thank you to my brilliantly talented nephew Seb Phd and amazingly confident niece Nadia, two of the wisest young people I know. Your advice has shaped my book in so many positive ways - *you are both destined for great things.* Thank you to the lovely Beth Jones for helping me to design the front cover of my book and the layout – you are a very clever young lady.

And to your amazingly wise Mum and my Mentor Nicky, who works so hard to support parents herself. To my lecturers Norma, Mary and Angela at Bristol's University of the West of England. Without their belief in me I wouldn't have had the courage to train as a Careers Adviser. *It is still the best job in the world after all these years.* To my Cousin Dave, a huge "thank you" for taking time to read my manuscript and for being so positive. You have encouraged me even when you have been so busy yourself - the mark of a true friend. And another to your clever colleague and Editor Gary Dalkin at www.tothelastword.com for offering such wise advice and really helped to shape Just Be Yourself. Thank you too to Keith from the Princes Trust for your enthusiasm and encouragement.

And to those special people who have offered me support and been so encouraging about my writing. To the wonderful author Rachel Kelly and Professors Victoria Door and Dave Putwain, I am so grateful for and humbled by your praise. And the inspirational Oliver Speight, founder of the amazing charity Sp8 of the Art, An incredibly brave man who inspired me to tell my own story. *If only all education could be as much fun as you have made it at Sp8.* To the young people I meet every week that amaze and inspire me by their resilience. I wish I could spare you some of the stress of almost continuous tests 🫱

Support, Advice & Inspiration

www.familylives.org.uk - *'Advice on all aspects of family life including development, parenting and relationship support, mental health concerns of both parents and their children'.*

On-line parenting course, parenting videos & free helpline: 0808 800 2222.

www.youngminds.org.uk *'Offering free, confidential online and telephone support. Information, training and advice to any adult worried about emotional problems, behaviour or mental health of a child or young person up to the age of 25'.* **The Young Minds Parents (free) Helpline 0808 802 5544**

www.sane.org.uk/support – **SANE** *provides emotional support to anyone affected by mental health problems, including families, friends and carers* - **Helpline**: 0300 304 7000 (4.30pm – 10.30pm every day) & Read my Blog on the SANE site.

NHS Moodzone: **https://www.nhs.uk › Health A-Z › Moodzone** *'Amazing help and advice to boost mental health'.*

https://www.wikihow.com/Develop-SelfEsteem
Easy to follow steps (with pictures) to build self-confidence.

www.empoweringparents.com

'Advice on coping with some of the most difficult behaviour issues parents face, with workable and brilliant strategies to use.'

www.kidscape.org.uk - *'providing children, families, carers and professionals with advice, training and practical tools to prevent bullying and protect young lives.'*

https://www.education.gov.uk/consultations - *'Make your feelings known on Government policies which directly affect your children and teens.'*

https://theconversation.com/scare-tacticson-failing-exams-can-lead-to-lower-grades By Professor Dave Putwain, AfBPS C.Psychol, Liverpool John Moores University – *How using encouragement rather than fear improves exam performance and self-esteem.*

www.teachers.org.uk/educationpolicies/research/examfactories - 2016 vital research carried out by the National Union of Teachers into the pressures in Education.

Developing Creative and Critical
Educational Practitioners - by Dr Victoria
Door. (ISBN: 9781909682375) from
Amazon's Book Store

Walking on Sunshine – 52 Small Steps to Happiness'
by Rachel Kelly & with illustrations by Jonathan Pugh
(Short Books 2015 ISBN-10: 1780722524)

How to Win Friends & Influence People by
Dale Carnegie (Revised 2006 by Vermilion)

The Power of Positive Thinking by Norman
Vincent Peale (Revised in 1990 by Cedar Books &
Vermilion)

Strength to Love by Martin Luther King (Collins 1970)

Poems of Maya Angelou (1980 - Bantam USA)

The Teenager Who Came to Tea by Josie Lloyd &
Emlyn Rees (Constable 2015) - '*A hilarious parody for
all the wonderful teenagers in our lives.*'

Support the wonderful charity CHICKS who offer free
holidays for disadvantaged young people :
https://chicks.org.uk/

Help With Career Ideas & Planning

Start with the BUZZ quiz to find out more about which job areas will 'match' your personality: www.icould.com/buzz Developed originally by the brilliant Carl Jung to explain different personality types. *Amazingly accurate & a great place to start* ☺

Then find out more about the jobs which are suggested for you, along with any others by using: www.careerpilot.org.uk/job-sectors. This site has easy to understand facts on job routes, opportunities and pay-scales. *A brilliant web site* ☺

If you have enjoyed '**Just be Yourself**' please get in touch at beingyou02@gmail.com

Follow my Blog too on the SANE website
&
Also available on Amazon as an eBook or in paperback & where you have the opportunity to leave feedback ☺

My very best wishes,

Ellen

x

Example School Charter

This code describes the sort of school we want and how we are going to make it work. As pupils and teachers we have the right to –

- LIVE IN A CLEAN ENVIRONMENT
  So treat rooms & furniture with respect
- LEARN & WORK IN A PRODUCTIVE WAY
  So work quietly and allow others to do so
- MOVE SAFELY AROUND THE SCHOOL
  So walk carefully & considerately
- ENJOY TALKING TO OTHER PEOPLE
  So avoid loud or offensive language

TREAT OTHERS AS YOU HOPE THEY WILL TREAT YOU & MAKE EVERY DAY A POSITIVE EXPERIENCE.

39523683R00040

Printed in Poland
by Amazon Fulfillment
Poland Sp. z o.o., Wrocław